Rendering South Africa Undesirable: A Critique of Refugee and Informal Sector Policy

Jonathan Crush, Caroline Skinner and Manal Stulgaitis

SAMP MIGRATION POLICY SERIES NO. 79

Series Editor: Prof. Jonathan Crush

Southern African Migration Programme (SAMP)
2017

AUTHORS

Jonathan Crush is CIGI Chair in Global Migration and Development, International Migration Research Centre, Balsillie School of International Affairs, Waterloo.

Caroline Skinner is a Senior Researcher at the African Centre for Cities, University of Cape Town, and Urban Policies Research Director of WIEGO.

Manal Stulgaitis is an Independent Consultant, Cape Town.

ACKNOWLEDGEMENTS

We wish to thank the UNHCR Geneva for funding SAMP's Refugee Economic Impacts project and the IDRC for its support of the SAMP Growing Informal Cities Project. Our thanks also to Vanya Gastrow, Godfrey Tawodzera, Bronwen Dachs and Sujata Ramachandran for their assistance.

Published by the Southern African Migration Programme, International Migration Research Centre, Balsillie School of International Affairs, Waterloo, Ontario, Canada samponline.org

First published 2017

ISBN 978-1-920596-40-8

Cover photo: Nikki Rixon / Twenty Ten / Africa Media Online

Production by Bronwen Dachs Muller, Cape Town

Printed by Print on Demand, Cape Town

CONTENTS   PAGE

EXECUTIVE SUMMARY

South Africa's rights-based refugee legislation has historically allowed refugees and asylum-seekers to access a broad array of rights from health services to education and employment. South Africa has never hosted a dedicated refugee camp or detention centre. Refugees and asylum-seekers have found their way into South Africa's social and economic fabric, sending their children to South African schools, finding employment in South African businesses and households, and establishing their own formal and informal businesses. The South African government has increasingly taken the position that the country's post-apartheid refugee protection legislation is too generous and needs to be revised with greater restrictions and fewer rights. This has resulted in major changes to the 1998 Refugees Act in the 2016 Refugees Amendment Act, and the indication of a new restrictive approach to refugee protection in the 2017 White Paper on International Migration in South Africa. Both developments seek to bring South Africa in line with the exclusionary policies towards asylum-seekers and refugees seen in many other countries globally. These developments, several years in the making, represent a profound reconfiguration of the country's approach to refugee rights, protections, and associated international obligations; moving away from an integration approach towards a containment and repulsion approach. This is part of a more global state-led trend, which seeks to inhibit access to the physical territory and refugee protection systems through erecting physical, economic and social barriers to entry.

In the absence of material support from the South African government or the UNHCR, one of the primary livelihood strategies of asylum-seekers and refugees in the country has been to create work for themselves in the informal sector. The policy environment in which refugee entrepreneurs run informal businesses on the streets and in residential areas is not governed by refugee legislation but by national, provincial and local policies towards the informal sector. Those working in the informal sector face an ambiguous policy environment that has occasionally supported but largely ignored, and at times actively destroyed, informal sector livelihoods and those of migrant and refugee businesses in particular. To fully understand the policy environment within which migrants and refugees establish and operate their enterprises in the South African informal sector, this report brings together two streams of policy analysis. The first concerns South Africa's changing refugee policies and practices and the erosion of the protective and progressive refugee policy approach that characterized the immediate post-apartheid period. The second concerns the highly ambiguous post-apartheid informal sector policy, which oscillates between tolerance and attempted destruction at national and municipal levels. While there have been longstanding tensions between foreign and South African informal sector operators, an overtly anti-foreign migrant sentiment has increasingly been expressed in official policy and practice.

INTRODUCTION

The past decade has seen South Africa's apparently generous asylum and refugee system flounder, characterized by ever-growing wait times for status decisions, increased barriers for application and renewal of permits, and growing disregard for refugee law and court orders.[1] The South African government has increasingly taken the position that the country's post-apartheid refugee protection legislation is far too generous and needs to be revised in the direction of greater restrictions and fewer rights. This has resulted in major changes to the 1998 Refugees Act in the 2016 Refugees Amendment Act, and the indication of a new restrictive approach to refugee protection in the 2017 White Paper on International Migration in South Africa.[2] Both developments seek to bring South Africa in line with the exclusionary policies towards asylum-seekers and refugees seen in many other countries globally.[3] In the absence of material support from the South African government or the UNHCR, one of the primary livelihood strategies of asylum-seekers and refugees in the country has been to create work for themselves in the informal sector. The policy environment in which refugee entrepreneurs run informal businesses on the streets and in residential areas is not governed by refugee legislation but by national, provincial and local policies towards the informal sector. Those working in the informal sector face an ambiguous policy environment that has occasionally supported but largely ignored, and at times actively destroyed, informal sector livelihoods and those of migrant and refugee businesses in particular.

To fully understand the policy environment within which migrants and refugees establish and operate their enterprises in the South African informal sector, we need to bring together two streams of policy analysis. The first concerns South Africa's changing refugee policies and practices and the erosion of the protective and progressive refugee policy approach that characterized the immediate post-apartheid period.[4] The second concerns the highly ambiguous post-apartheid informal sector policy, which oscillates between tolerance and attempted destruction at national and municipal levels. While there have been longstanding tensions between foreign and South African informal sector operators, an overtly anti-foreign migrant sentiment has increasingly been expressed in official policy and practice.

This report underlines the need for both a rights-based asylum system and more progressive policies towards the informal sector. Refugee entrepreneurs and service providers agree that obtaining refugee status is key to enabling refugee entrepreneurship and sustainable livelihoods. While this status should mark a signpost to successful local integration, the South African government continues to pile on administrative and logistical barriers to the asylum process and prospective refugees. These measures add to the ambiguity around migration management in the country and complicate the prospects for refugees to provide for themselves in a safe and sustainable manner.

The report is based on a review of media and official government sources, published and grey literature, and interviews with key informants in the city of Cape Town and the provinces of Limpopo and Gauteng during 2015. A total of 30 in-depth interviews were conducted including with researchers, refugee and diaspora associations, refugee rights NGOs, law enforcement, the City of Cape Town and Western Cape governments, and international organizations such as the IOM and UNHCR. Interviews were also conducted with national government departments including Home Affairs, Labour, and Small Business Development.

REFUGEE POLICY AND PRACTICE

South Africa is a signatory to the 1951 United Nations Convention on the Status of Refugees and the 1969 OAU Convention Governing the Specific Aspects of Refugee Problems in Africa. Since the end of apartheid, it has built a reputation as a protective and progressive refugee-receiving country. South Africa's 1998 Refugees Act integrated international refugee protections into domestic law and exceeded international standards in important respects. The Act made generous allowances for freedom of movement, access to health and education services, some social protection, and the right to work. Most notably, it Act embraced local integration over encampment, which was a progressive choice in Africa at the time.[5] Underpinning the Act was a political and ideological approach which posited that refugees were permitted and fully expected to integrate temporarily into the host country and benefit from all attendant protections and rights granted to citizens by the Constitution. Refugees who had been in the country for five years were entitled to apply for permanent residence. In exchange for these progressive policies, both government and the UNHCR incurred minimal costs in providing material support for asylum-seekers and refugees in the country.

In the years since these somewhat idealistic beginnings, South Africa has seen a distinct deterioration in the rights-based approach to refugee protection.[6] International praise for South Africa's liberal approach has been eroded by chronic processing delays, poor and ill-informed adjudication, and the corruption and mismanagement that has become endemic to the asylum process. South Africa has one of the longest asylum adjudication periods in the world, with some cases stretching out for many years. After 2007, the economic meltdown in Zimbabwe imposed significant pressure on the asylum system as migrants from Zimbabwe moved in large numbers to South Africa.[7] South Africa's failure to anticipate and account for the entry of Zimbabweans created a situation whereby the asylum system became contorted into something of a "catch all" for generalized migration into South Africa.[8] While Zimbabwean migrants have subsequently been criticized by the South African government for "abusing" and overloading the asylum process, they had no other options for legal stay in South Africa. They were in fact encouraged to use the system by the establishment of a Refugee Reception Office in Musina by the Department of Home Affairs (DHA), specifically to speed up the issue of asylum-seeker permits to Zimbabweans.

Those close to the process argue that the demand for a place in South Africa's asylum queue, with its attendant right to work, rendered the system ineffectual in conducting legitimate refugee adjudication. This translated into increasingly strident denunciations of "bogus" claimants and "abuse of the system" by economic migrants. As the Minister of Home Affairs observed in a speech on World Refugee Day in 2016: "An unintended consequence of our liberal asylum regime has been that migrants who are not genuine refugees but are seeking economic opportunities have used it to attempt to regularise their stay in South Africa. The sheer volume of applications from these migrants has placed an enormous burden on the refugee status determination process, which has disadvantaged genuine asylum seekers by delaying their decisions, in the past taking years where they should take no more than 6 months".[9] The official line is that 90% of asylum-seekers are economic migrants, although there is no evidential basis for this claim (other than the fact that only about 10% of asylum-seekers to date have been granted refugee status).[10] However, this conclusion is a *non-sequitur*, given the arbitrariness of many decisions and the practice of adjudicating claims by country or origin and not the personal experience of the individual claimant.[11] The fact that the rejection rate is also a function of a system that is under-resourced, staffed by small numbers of poorly trained officers and rife with corruption, is unacknowledged.

The reasons for this shift from rights and protections towards exclusion and control are seen by some as the inevitable consequence of life in a country where the majority still struggle to meet basic needs and there is competition for scarce public resources such as education, health care, and shelter, as well as employment and other livelihood opportunities.[12] In this zero sum game, every advantage that a refugee or asylum-seeker enjoys necessarily disadvantages a South African. However, at least one recent study has argued that South Africans do not oppose refugee protection for reasons of economic self-interest.[13] Rather their opposition is further evidence of the xenophobic character of South African society, with the attendant failure to acknowledge the positive economic, social and cultural contribution that refugees and asylum-seekers make to the country.[14] As the study concludes, "public animosity towards refugees in South Africa has motivated anti-immigrant riots, violence, and prejudice which has negatively impacted on refugee protection."[15] As a result, "a protection strategy dedicated to maximizing refugees' freedom and integration may prove politically untenable in an era of pronounced anti-immigrant hostilities."[16]

Government argues that the breakdown of the refugee protection system in South Africa, and the need for reform, is because it has been overwhelmed by economic migrants. For a period, the DHA argued that there were a million asylum-seekers in the country, a figure that was uncritically reproduced by the UNHCR and the media and translated into bogus claims that South Africa was the leading global destination for refugees. The White Paper on International Migration admits that this figure is erroneous, noting that in 2015, only 78,339 asylum-seeker (Section 22) permits were still active.[17] This revised figure is a considerable climb-down by the DHA and hardly justifies the image it promulgated of a system swamped.[18] Nor does it justify the draconian amendments to the law in process. Rather than being motivated by a need to address an overburdened system, therefore, the narrowing of refugee rights and imposition of additional limitations on the ability of refugees to find safety and security in South Africa are better interpreted as an effort to make the country an undesirable destination for asylum-seekers and refugees. Several inter-connected strategies have been developed to achieve this end. All are embodied in the 2016 Refugees Amendment Act (which was passed Parliament in March 2017 and awaits Cabinet approval before becoming law) and the 2017 White Paper on International Migration.

The first strategy has been to shift from an integrationist towards a detention model. The White Paper on International Migration reaffirms plans that are already under way to establish what it calls Asylum-Seeker Processing Centres away from urban areas.[19] These are widely seen by critics as a euphemism for encampment despite government denials.

Plans have been drawn up for the location and physical infrastructure of detention centres close to South Africa's borders with Zimbabwe and Mozambique and construction has apparently begun on a detention centre at Lebombo.[20] The White Paper notes that these detention centres are intended to accommodate all asylum-seekers during their status determination process.[21] Freedom of movement and integration into local communities (as at present) would be halted. So-called "low risk" asylum-seekers might be released into the care of national or international organizations and family or community members who would have to provide guarantees of support that excluded employment. Asylum-seekers would be deprived of the court-mandated right they have at present to work or study "since their basic needs will be catered for in the processing centres."[22] To pre-empt the inevitable, and justifiable, criticism that South Africa is introducing a policy of encampment, the earlier Green Paper awkwardly asserted that "these centres should not be considered as contrary to the policy of non-encampment but as centres for mitigating security risks posed by irregular migration" (DHA, 2016: 66). The claim that this somehow represents a continuation of the country's non-encampment policy is disingenuous. Under this policy, asylum-seekers will be sequestered in detention centres for the duration of the adjudication process, which is unrealistically envisioned as a 60 to 90-day process. Whether that process takes place within the proposed period or not, asylum-seekers would be fully dependent on government or international organizations for food, shelter, health care, education and other basic needs. The cost of constructing and maintaining detention centres for large numbers of asylum-seekers will be massive and UNHCR has indicated that it will not underwrite detention costs despite appeals from the South African government (which previously constrained the UNHCR from offering material assistance to asylum-seekers). If South Africa faced an influx of asylum-seekers in the future akin to the over 200,000 Zimbabweans between 2006 and 2009, it is difficult to see how these centres would cope.

The second major strategy to turn the country into an undesirable destination for refugees is to put in place procedural, administrative and logistical hurdles that complicate an already tenuous status and sustainability. The most obvious example is the Department of Home Affairs halving the number of Refugee Reception Offices (RROs) in the country by closing busy offices in Johannesburg (Crown Mines), Cape Town and Port Elizabeth. Only three RROs remain open: in Musina, Durban and Pretoria. The closure was "not merely a technical, operational decision, but one which impacts on the basic principles of the asylum system, namely access (for initial applications, renewals, status determination interviews and appeals) and administrative efficiency and fairness."[23] Legal challenges to the closures have produced contradictory outcomes. The Supreme Court of Appeal ordered the re-opening of the Port Elizabeth RRO, a judgment that the DHA has been slow to implement. In contrast, the Cape Town High Court decided that the Cape Town RRO could remain closed. Because of the controversy, the 2016 Refugees Amendment Act gives the Director General of Home Affairs new powers to "dis-establish" any RRO and to force a whole category of asylum-seeker (defined in terms of country of origin or "a particular gender, religion, nationality, political opinion or social group") to report at designated RROs.

The associated administrative requirement that asylum-seekers must renew their permits every one to six months at the RRO where they obtained their permit (rather than an ordinary Home Affairs Office) imposes considerable financial and other hardships. The renewal period appears to be arbitrary and, according to some refugees, depends on the size of the bribe that they are willing to pay. Individuals and families who have found safety, shelter, work or school in another part of the country are forced to travel to the RRO to ensure that their status remains intact. Furthermore, wait times for receiving or renewing a permit are considerable. The scene outside the Marabastad (Pretoria) RRO was described by one key informant as follows:

> They come to Pretoria, there are queues and queues, never-ending queues. And then each country has a day. So now you have come to the Home Affairs office and it's not your turn, your turn only comes after 4 days. And then you are told that if you have ZAR2,000, these officials walk around and if you have money, you give them the money and go to the front of the queue. If you don't have money, then you are right at the back. And then you have to come back the following week on the day of your country.

In a situation where asylum-seekers are almost exclusively self-supporting, without the assistance of government or the international community, they are forced to sacrifice valuable time and money, risk jeopardizing their jobs, and have to travel with or leave young children behind. Under the 2016 Act, failure to renew an asylum-seeker permit within one month of expiry will lead to automatic revocation of status, forfeiture of the right to renewal, and treatment as an "illegal foreigner" in terms of the Immigration Act (that is, summary arrest and deportation). Asylum-seekers whose claims are refused are also to be treated as "illegal foreigners". An asylum-seeker with an expired permit will also be guilty of an offence and liable to a fine and imprisonment of up to five years or both. Any individual or group of asylum-seekers or refugees can be arrested and deported on the vaguely-worded grounds of "national interest or public order."

The third strategy to undermine the rights of asylum-seekers and refugees and to make South Africa an undesirable place of refuge, is to undercut court judgments affirming the right of asylum-seekers and refugees to employment and self-employment. The 2016 Act explicitly seeks to overturn a judgment that permitted asylum-seekers to work in South Africa while awaiting adjudication of their claims. The onus will now be on "family and friends" to support asylum-seekers for their first four months in the country. If such support is not available, the UNHCR and NGOs are permitted to provide "shelter and basic necessities." In both situations, the asylum-seeker is prohibited from working, while government assumes no responsibility for their care and protection. The government-appointed Standing Committee on Refugee Affairs is also empowered to decide unilaterally under what conditions asylum-seekers may work or study. If they are permitted to work or study, they are required to provide a letter from the employer or institution within 14 days from the date of employment or enrolment. The employer or institution can be fined ZAR20,000 if they fail to provide the documentation in the prescribed period. The right to work can also be revoked by the Director General. The Act says nothing about the right to access informal work and self-employment, which was a key component of earlier court judgments.

The fourth strategy in rendering South Africa undesirable is to ensure that protection is always temporary by making it extremely difficult for refugees to progress to permanent residence and eventual citizenship. The 1998 Act stated that refugees were entitled to apply for permanent residence after five years' continuous residence in South Africa and refugees "of good and sound character" could be issued with permanent residence permits irrespective of the length of sojourn in the country. This is one reason why the maximum length of a refugee (Section 24) permit was four years. The 2016 Act gives the Minister of Home Affairs new powers to issue an order that ceases recognition of an individual refugee or group of refugees or to revoke refugee status without the obligation to provide justification for such an action. The right of a refugee to apply for permanent residence has also been extended from five to 10 years. The White Paper proposes to do away with the category of permanent residence altogether and replace it with a long-term, renewable residence visa, for which refugees would become eligible after 10 years. It also seeks to sever any connection between length of residence and citizenship eligibility.[24]

The recent case of long-term Angolan refugees in South Africa provides an instructive example of the official thinking underlying the current drive to choke the refugee path to permanent residence. In 2013, the Department of Home Affairs stripped all refugees from

Angola of their refugee status irrespective of length of residence and then, under protest, issued them with two-year non-renewable temporary residence permits (called Angolan Cessation Permits or ACPs).[25] In 2016, after extensive negotiations between human rights advocates and the DHA, the department finally agreed that former Angolan refugees could apply for permanent residence. The Western Cape High Court then issued an order by which all former Angolan refugees with expired ACPs could apply for permanent residence. In February 2017, the Scalabrini Centre of Cape Town submitted 1,757 applications on behalf of Angolan refugees to the DHA. The successful court action not only prevents the summary deportation of former Angolan refugees but could potentially provide an important precedent for future cases of cessation. The White Paper attempts to ensure that this will never happen.

Finally, prior to 2010, the Financial Intelligence Centre Act (FICA) prohibited refugees and asylum-seekers from opening bank accounts in South Africa. That policy was later relaxed but FICA's anti-money-laundering provisions still require banks to verify the identity of persons wanting to open a bank account. Banks are given wide discretion as to how they implement the requirements, with the result that many refuse to open accounts for refugees and asylum-seekers. In response to legal action, the DHA and FICA agreed that the department would provide banks with the means to verify the authenticity of refugee and asylum permits. In practice, opening a bank account remains a challenge for refugees and asylum-seekers, with banks remaining distrustful of DHA documentation. There have also been instances of refugees and asylum-seekers having their assets frozen when identity documents have not been renewed on time, when identity documents change, or when the DHA has failed to respond to verification enquiries in a timely manner. A frozen bank account raises grave protection concerns, threatening the ability to pay rent, buy food, care for children, and even cover costs for long-distance travel for the purposes of renewing status documentation.[26] Because of these difficulties, refugees and asylum-seekers tend to carry large amounts of cash, making them ready targets for theft. Refugees and asylum-seekers also find it extremely difficult to obtain bank loans to start a business or for ongoing operations. Only 1% had managed to secure a bank loan to start a business in a recent SAMP survey of over 1,000 refugee-owned informal businesses. The refusal rate was 75%-80%. While it would be incorrect to suggest that banks are colluding in the project to make South Africa an undesirable destination, their actions certainly have that effect.

INFORMAL SECTOR POLICY AND PRACTICE

Most asylum-seekers and refugees have little choice but to work in the informal sector in South Africa. If the proposals to prohibit asylum-seekers from working legally become law, this will have a major impact on the sector. A 2015 SAMP survey of 1,132 informal businesses run by migrants in Cape Town and Johannesburg found that 18% were refugee (Section 24) permit holders and 30% were asylum-seeker (Section 22) permit holders.[27] Depriving asylum-seekers (present and future) of the right to self-employment in the informal sector will undoubtedly lead to further court challenges but the intent is clearly to reduce the number of asylum-seekers coming to South Africa and the number of foreign-owned enterprises in the sector. This would be consistent with the general aim of rendering South Africa an undesirable destination, but would also further national and local informal sector policy. These policies are increasingly focused on demonizing non-South Africans and forcing them off the streets and out of the low-income communities where they play a central role in making food and other consumables accessible to the urban poor.

Under apartheid, black South Africans were forbidden from engaging in informal businesses and access to business premises was strictly regulated. Influx control laws became increasingly unenforceable in the mid-1980s and were abolished in 1986. In 1987, the National White Paper on Privatisation and Deregulation introduced a more tolerant approach to black small business as part of a broader new economic philosophy informed by the Reagan-Thatcher era of deregulation. The change of attitude culminated in the Businesses Act 71 of 1991 (which repealed numerous restrictive laws and secured a more liberal approach to business licencing, premises and hours for both formal and informal business). This legislation was a key measure for removing barriers to the operation of informal activities and was, in effect, a complete reversal of the apartheid approach.

After the passage of the 1991 Act, informal-sector activities increased in all cities and towns. Local authorities, however, complained that they were unable to cope, particularly with the growth of informal trading in public spaces. This led to the Businesses Amendment Act 186 of 1993 which gave provinces the discretion to develop their own legislation and allowed local authorities to formulate street-trading bylaws, and declare restricted and prohibited trade zones. Since then, local authorities across the country have promulgated such bylaws in near mirror images of one another. In all major metropoles, the sanctions for violation were inappropriately criminalized – either a fine or imprisonment – indicating a punitive approach to informal sector management.

At a national level, the 1995 White Paper on the Development and Promotion of Small Businesses was one of the first economic policy initiatives of the post-apartheid government. The White Paper and the legislation that stemmed from it – the 1996 National Small Business Act – acknowledged survivalist and micro-enterprises as components of small business, thus making them, on paper, beneficiaries of government support. Both documents were, however, silent on the specific needs of these smaller players, suggesting that the role played by this group was not seen as a critical issue. Neither referred to foreign migrants or refugees, possibly because their presence in the small business sector was fairly small at the time. To implement the new approach, the Department of Trade and Industry (DTI) set up the Ntsika Enterprise Promotion Agency as a facilitation and promotion body for small businesses and Khula Finance to secure small-business access to financial services. It also supported the establishment of a countrywide network of Local Business Development Centres to provide non-financial support to small, medium and micro enterprises (SMMEs).

In 2004, a comprehensive review of the impact of the post-apartheid SMME programmes concluded that "existing government SMME programmes largely have been biased towards the groups of small and medium-sized enterprises and to a large extent have by-passed micro-enterprises and the informal economy."[28] An evaluation of the government's skills development system concluded similarly that those working in the informal sector had "fallen into the gap" between small businesses and the unemployed.[29] These findings were echoed in an informal-sector budget analysis and confirmed by survey data conducted with informal-sector operators in Johannesburg and Durban.[30]

In 2003, President Mbeki publicly advocated for the idea of the "second economy" in an address to the National Council of Provinces. Mbeki's negative view of the second economy saw it as characterized by "underdevelopment, contributes little to GDP, contains a large percentage of our population, incorporates the poorest of our rural and urban poor, is structurally disconnected from both the first and the global economy, and is incapable of self-generated growth and development."[31] According to Mbeki, the second economy required "the infusion of capital and other resources by the democratic state to ensure the integration of this economy within the developed sector." Although the concept of a second economy was not novel, its application to South Africa was an important moment in raising the public policy profile of the informal sector. The whole idea of a second economy elicited a flurry of criticism, however.[32] According to one critic, second-economy arguments were based on the premise that "the mainstream of the economy is working rather well, and government action is needed to enhance the linkages between the first and second economy and where appropriate to provide relief, such as public works programmes, to those locked into the informal economy."[33]

Subsequent policy pronouncements argued that the second economy should be eradicated altogether. The 2006 Accelerated Shared Growth Initiative of South Africa, for example, called for the "elimination" of the second economy.[34] In 2008, the Presidency initiated the Second Economy Strategy Project, which proposed the progressive incorporation of the second into the first economy. The project's strategic framework and strategies were approved by Cabinet but the recall of Mbeki as President led to a loss of momentum. While a proposed community works programme was implemented, the remaining strategies were not translated into activities at national, provincial and local levels.

Since 2012, increasing attention has been paid to the informal sector at national level – albeit in a somewhat haphazard and uncoordinated fashion. Different initiatives represent simultaneous neglect, support and suppression. The 2012 National Development Plan (NDP), for example, assigns a large role to small businesses in its employment scenarios and plans.[35] The NDP's ideal scenario projects that 11 million jobs will be created by 2030, suggesting that 90% of these new jobs will be created by small and growing enterprises. Of these, the informal sector (and domestic work) will create between 1.2 million and 2.1 million new jobs.[36] However, the NDP chapter on the economy says nothing about strategies for the informal sector *per se*, how existing operators in the informal sector will be supported, and how barriers to entry will be addressed to help generate new jobs.

Also in 2012, the DTI established a new directorate for Informal Business and Chamber Support. This constituted a recognition by the DTI of the role of the informal sector in broadening economic participation.[37] By the end of the year, the directorate had established a reference group charged with developing a National Informal Business Development Strategic Framework. Under the guidance of the reference group, DTI staff conducted consultations with stakeholders in the informal sector, formal business, and local government officials over a few months, and reported back to the reference group in February 2013. This led to the launch of the National Informal Business Upliftment Strategy (NIBUS) in 2014.[38] In the same period, and apparently unbeknown to the reference group, another section of the DTI was working under the Minister's direction on new legislation to replace the Businesses Amendment Act of 1993.

In March 2013, the DTI released a draft Business Licensing Bill.[39] The Bill's stated aim was "to provide for a simple and enabling framework for procedures for application of business licences by setting norms and standards."[40] The DTI Minister, Rob Davies, later claimed that the Bill was put in place to deal with illegal trading practices, citing illegal imports, sub-standard goods, counterfeit goods, and illegal drug and liquor trading. In fact, as critics pointed out, these were already adequately dealt with through other laws such as the Customs and Excise Act of 1964, the Foodstuffs, Cosmetics, and Disinfectants Act of 1972, Counterfeit Goods Act of 1997, Drugs and Drug Trafficking Act of 1992 and a raft of provincial level legislation aimed at regulating (through the issuing of licences) informal liquor outlets or shebeens.[41]

Where the NIBUS and the draft Business Licensing Bill converge is their common attitude towards migrants and refugees running small businesses in the informal economy. Essentially, both attempt to regulate, control and exclude participation by non-South Africans. The NIBUS is characterized by implicit and explicit anti-migrant sentiment. It states that foreign-owned informal businesses are an "express challenge" since there is "no regulatory restrictions in controlling the influx of foreigners (sic)" and "no synergy between the DTI and Home Affairs in devising strategies and policies to control foreign business activities."[42] It identifies a supposed "foreign trader challenge" in the informal sector, noting that "there is evidence of violence and unhappiness of local communities with regard to the *takeover* of local business by foreign nationals" [our emphasis].[43] There are numerous complementary suggestions to strengthen South African informal sector businesses. To reduce the "xenophobia associated with foreign national traders," the NIBUS proposes to "influence the type of businesses that foreign nationals should run and the demarcated areas where these businesses should be active."[44] As precedent for an exclusionary policy, NIBUS cites the Ghana Investment Promotion Centre Act, which has reserved selling at markets, petty trading and hawking, and the operation of metered taxis, car hire services, beauty salons and barber shops to nationals only, as well as India and Malaysia's restrictions on foreign economic participation.[45] The Department of Home Affairs is also criticized for supposedly having "no regulatory restrictions in controlling the influx of foreigners."[46] One assessment concluded that "NIBUS is a pro-development approach for South African informal entrepreneurs which is allied to an anti-developmental agenda towards migrant entrepreneurs."[47] In 2013, the Deputy Minister of Trade and Industry sharply criticized South Africans for renting their properties to migrants, saying that "the scourge of South

Africans in townships selling and renting their businesses to foreigners unfortunately does not assist us as government in our efforts to support and grow these informal businesses."[48]

Turning to the draft Business Licensing Bill, the legislation would require anyone involved in business activities – no matter how small – to have a licence with fines or imprisonment for up to 10 years for those in contravention. Foreign migrants would only be licensed if they had business permits, which, according to the 2002 Immigration Act, have to be applied for in the country of origin and are only granted if the applicant can demonstrate having ZAR2.5 million to invest in South Africa. The Bill suggested that wide-ranging discretionary powers be given to both the licensing authority and inspectors, far greater than those granted by the 1993 Business Amendment Act. The eventual withdrawal of the Bill from Parliament was prompted not by concerns about its draconian approach to migrants and refugees in the sector, but because of a chorus of opposition from private business and non-governmental organizations pointing out that the result would be large-scale criminalizing of the informal sector as a whole. A submission from StreetNet International, on behalf of South African street trader organizations from all nine provinces, was particularly critical: "What the [1991] Businesses Act added to the new South Africa was a developmental approach…instead of the old abolitionist approach which characterised the Apartheid era. We believe that the repeal of the Businesses Act and replacement with this Bill…would take us back to the era of forced removals."[49]

The impossible conditions imposed on migrants and refugees for accessing a licence would have meant that few migrant informal operators would qualify and most would therefore be criminalized. Indeed, it has been argued that the Bill was introduced to regulate foreign migrants out of the sector in the interests of their South African counterparts.[50] To understand the anti-migrant content of the NIBUS and Draft Bill, it is important to appreciate the upsurge of animosity towards refugees and asylum-seekers among South African-owned businesses.[51] Both can be seen as a policy response to the complaints of these operators and the pressure on government to act. They can also be seen as a response to the phenomenon of "violent entrepreneurship"; that is, South Africans taking the law into their own hands and organizing attacks on refugee businesses. Instead of offering and providing protection to those at risk, the DTI reached the conclusion that it would be better to adopt the xenophobic rhetoric of the streets, cast refugees and asylum-seekers as a threat, and implement policies to try to get them out of the informal sector. These attitudes and responses to refugees and asylum-seekers in the informal sector were certainly not confined to the DTI and DHA, and became particularly apparent in the response to a wave of violent xenophobic attacks in early 2015.

The major government response to the 2015 violence was the establishment of an Inter-Ministerial Committee on Migration (IMC) housed in the Presidency, on which 15 government ministers sat. The IMC concluded that the primary cause of the violence against foreign nationals was "increased competition arising from the socio-economic circumstances in South Africa."[52] The total number of migrants in the country was grossly exaggerated at between five million and six million. It was thus "highly likely" that immigrants represented more than 10% of the country's population. Foreign nationals were supposedly placing a strain on government services such as health, housing, education and social grants and "dominating trade in certain sectors such as consumable goods in informal settlements which has had a negative impact on unemployed and low skilled South Africans." The IMC also referred to the "business models used by migrants to discourage competition such as forming monopolies, evading taxes, avoiding customs and selling illegal and expired goods."[53]

In April 2015, the IMC launched the nationwide Operation Fiela. Billed as a crime-fighting initiative, a central component of the operation was a massive drive to harass migrant-owned businesses, locate undocumented migrants and facilitate their deportation. In Cape Town, for example, just before the global celebration of World Refugee Day, the police, army, traffic officials, and immigration officials descended on Cape Town's station deck (a taxi terminus and market above Cape Town's main railway station) and systematically harassed foreign-owned businesses:

> It was really terrifying the manner in which they did [things] yesterday. Soldiers pointed guns, ready to shoot anyone [who was] against what was happening. I was selling some brand stuff, but these people went beyond that. Some of them were wicked. I could neither question their authority nor do anything to stop them from taking my stuff. They came in and took down all my stuff. They confiscated almost 50 items [including] jeans, trousers and tops. Out of these items, less than ten were brand names. Yesterday was a great loss, since the operation went into our busiest time of the day, between 10 and 11am…The unfortunate thing is they did not give us a receipt to show what they have confiscated…I believe in a normal situation they issue a receipt…We did not get any chance to talk to them regarding how we could go about [getting back] the goods seized.[54]

By the end of 2015, government boasted that Operation Fiela had searched 460,000 people, 151,000 vehicles and 38,000 premises. The absence of due process in the militaristic implementation of Operation Fiela led Lawyers for Human Rights to (unsuccessfully) challenge the constitutionality of the operation in the North Gauteng High Court. An application for leave to appeal to the Constitutional Court was dismissed in December 2016. A representative for Lawyers for Human Rights described Operation Fiela as follows:

> *What we found astonishing was the Operation Fiela response from government. They said the appropriate response (to xenophobia) is multi-agency enforcement to identify and address and detain and deport undocumented migrants and the justification was that South Africans are concerned about large numbers of undocumented migrants and involvement in crime and threats to social cohesion. So the best way to address the issue was to remove them. It emphasised the growing securitisation of migration – the language they used was national security language and moved away from rights language.*

With regard, specifically, to the violence against foreign-owned businesses, government has been extremely responsive to arguments that these businesses are providing "unfair" competition and putting South Africans out of business. Whether this is true or not has never been ascertained and research evidence about the positive economic impacts of migrant and refugee business activity is strategically ignored.

In 2014, a Department of Small Business Development was hived off from the DTI to identify a strategy to manage the informal sector and encourage SMME development. The new Minister initially acknowledged the right of international migrants to operate when she stated that "they must make a living. The more they make a living, the more they contribute to the economy. They pay taxes and are active participants in the economy."[55] This quickly changed to an emphasis on the negative impacts on South Africans of "foreigners." By 2015, for example, she was castigating "foreign business owners" for expecting to co-exist peacefully with local business owners while not sharing their "trade secrets." She remarked that "foreigners" cannot "barricade themselves in and not share their practices with local business owners."[56] The adviser to the Minister speaks openly of the "invasion" of "foreign traders" as an "ongoing sore point."[57] Further, "foreigners have taken over these markets and even control sectors, such as hair dressing and value chains. Thus, the inter-mittent explosions against foreigners will continue despite efforts by the government to pacify the situation. Nobody wants this violence but, let us be frank with each other, locals are not merely going to sit in the corner and sulk."[58]

Recasting refugees and asylum-seekers as "foreigners" is key to this exclusionary discourse. At provincial government level, the national-level antagonism towards refugees and migrants in the informal sector has been repeated. While the 1993 amendment to the Businesses Act empowered provinces to develop dedicated provincial business acts, to date no province has done that. In KwaZulu-Natal (KZN), an informal economy policy process was initiated in 2003. This resulted, after eight years, in the KZN Informal Economy Policy of 2011, but it has not yet been developed into a White Paper.[59] In other provinces, reference is made to the informal sector in local economic development strategies (as in Limpopo) as well as township development strategies. The Western Cape promulgated its first dedicated Informal Sector Framework in 2014 and Gauteng recently released the Gauteng Informal Business Development Strategy.[60] Both focus on aligning with the NIBUS. All of the documents echo the need for financial and non-financial support to informal businesses (especially through small-business development centres), supporting informal trading in townships, improved access to business-related infrastructure facilities, and reviewing regulations and bylaws to support the informal business sector. However, there is a clear anti-foreign sentiment in the Gauteng strategy:

> *The existing competition for trading permits among local and foreign nationals is evident. Unfortunately, there are no regulatory restrictions in controlling the influx of foreign nationals. The Departments of Trade and Industry and Home Affairs should assist the province in devising strategies and policies to control foreign business activities.*[61]

Similar sentiments are expressed in the Western Cape document (Western Cape Province, 2014: 46). In KwaZulu-Natal, the provincial government formed and funded the KZN Provincial Association of Traders and traders' training academies. The purpose of this initiative is to "bring back our general dealer stores that used to be seen in our townships and villages (which) have been sold to foreign nationals."[62]

The provincial government in Limpopo Province has perhaps taken the most overtly hostile approach to migrants and refugees working in the informal sector. In 2012, it launched Operation Hardstick, an aggressive military-style campaign that targeted small informal businesses run by migrants and refugees. The Somali Association of South Africa supported by Lawyers for Human Rights contested the action in the courts. Court documents show that despite being labelled a crime-fighting initiative, Operation Hardstick was selectively enforced, affecting only migrant entrepreneurs and not South African businesses in the same locations.[63] Police shuttered over 600 businesses, detained owners, confiscated stock, imposed fines for trading without permits, and verbally abused the owners. Affected business owners were informed that "foreigners" were not allowed to operate in South Africa, that their asylum-seeker and refugee permits did not entitle them to run a business, and that they should leave the area. Thirty displaced migrants from Ethiopia were forced to flee when the house they had taken refuge in was fire-bombed.

The Supreme Court noted that police actions "tell a story of the most naked form of xenophobic discrimination and of the utter desperation experienced by the victims of that discrimination."[64] It also observed that "one is left with the uneasy feeling that the stance adopted by the authorities in relation to the licensing of spaza shops and tuck-shops was in order to induce foreign nationals who were destitute to leave our shores."[65] The court ruled in favour of the Somali Association and effectively established the right to self-employment for all asylum-seekers and refugees. Opposing the appeal were all three tiers of government – national, provincial and municipal – including the Limpopo Member of the Executive Council for Safety, Security and Liaison, the Provincial Commissioner of Police, the National Police Commissioner, the Standing Committee on Refugee Affairs, the Ministers of Police, Labour and Home Affairs, and two municipalities.

At city level, there is a preoccupation with the most visible element of the informal sector – street vendors – who operate in public spaces over which there are often competing interests. Policy statements on street trading or the informal sector show that, on paper, the positive contribution of the informal sector is sometimes recognised. In its street trading policy, the City of Johannesburg, for example, states that "informal trading is a positive development in the micro business sector as it contributes to the creation of jobs and alleviation of poverty and has the potential to expand further the City's economic base."[66] The City of Cape Town's policy advocates a "thriving informal trading sector that is valued and integrated into the economic life, urban landscape and social activities."[67] The eThekwini Informal Economy policy asserts that the "informal economy makes an important contribution to the economic and social life of Durban."[68] Despite the positive rhetoric, city-level actions reveal an ambivalent, if not actively hostile, approach to street traders.[69] In Johannesburg, this culminated in a draconian action in 2013 when the City Council ordered the removal of about 6,000 inner-city street traders, many of them migrants and refugees, in Operation Clean Sweep.[70] A group of traders took the City to court and the Constitutional Court ruled in their favour. Acting Chief Justice Moseneke stated that Operation Clean Sweep was an act of "humiliation and degradation" and that the City's attitude "may well border on the cynical."[71] Traders returned to the streets but in more limited numbers with the City declaring large inner city areas restricted and prohibited trade zones.

A recent analysis of Cape Town's approach to street traders shows systematic restriction and exclusion from the inner-city.[72] Township trading is also characterized by long-term neglect. In Khayelitsha, the city council had invested very little in infrastructure for street traders and had devolved the management of street trading to a small group of traders, with negative consequences for many others.[73] Although the policy environment in Cape Town varies across the city and between segments of the informal economy, "the modernist vision of a 'world-class city' with its associated antipathy to informality dominates, and informal space and activity is pathologized."[74] Migrants and refugees face additional challenges. In an interview for this study, the Cape Town Department of Economic Development claimed that "the City, in terms of its policy around trading, doesn't differentiate and we don't discriminate. There's set criteria in terms of who qualifies (for a trading bay and permit) and how that person qualifies. We don't look at what nationality the person is." But, as the interviewed official admitted, the City is forced to discriminate in practice because refugees have to produce documentation that South Africans do not. As indicated earlier, the renewal process for asylum and refugee permits is extremely unpredictable in terms of wait times and length granted. One way around this challenge is for South Africans to obtain the permit and then rent the space to refugees at a profit.

The regulation of Somali refugee spaza shops in Cape Town has involved various formal regulatory attempts to control and curtail the operations of Somali businesses including fines, drafting new by-laws, issuing policy statements about foreign shops, and proposing laws to tighten the regulation of the spaza market.[75] Both formal and informal measures skirt the law, are applied in a discriminatory manner, and stifle free competition. Mediation efforts led by the police and non-governmental organizations have culminated in agreements prohibiting the opening of new Somali shops in certain areas. The City certainly appears to be protecting the interests of South African spaza shop owners over their foreign counterparts.

Durban was once hailed for its relatively liberal stance on the informal sector.[76] A progressive informal-sector policy was unanimously accepted by the City Council in 2001 and remains official policy. The Council's actions reflect a more ambivalent approach, however. For example, a council-approved shopping mall development at the inner-city Warwick Junction transport node threatened 6,000 traders operating there and was only halted by a legal challenge.[77] In 2013, traders in both the inner city and outlying areas identified harassment by the police as their key business challenge.[78] In 2015, traders won a legal case challenging the constitutionality of confiscating their goods, forcing the City to redraft the street-trader by-laws. Again, court action proved to be the only way to secure relief.

CONCLUSION

Distinct from many other refugee-receiving countries, South Africa's rights-based refugee legislation has historically allowed for refugees and asylum-seekers to access a broad array of rights, from health services to education and employment. South Africa has never hosted a dedicated refugee camp or detention centre. In this environment, refugees and asylum-seekers have independently found their way into South Africa's social and economic fabric, sending their children to South African schools, finding employment in South African businesses and households, and establishing their own formal and informal businesses. The 2016 Amendment Act and 2017 White Paper are clear evidence of a new and less generous policy direction which is intended to shrink asylum space and further constrain the rights and protections afforded to refugees and asylum-seekers. The White Paper at least acknowledges that the existing policy framework unnecessarily criminalizes migrants from other SADC countries and does propose a set of quota-driven work and trading permits for these migrants, based on recommendations from one of the authors. Whether these proposals will pass muster in a crippling xenophobic environment remains to be seen.

Cumulatively, however, the changes documented in this paper illustrate a significant shift in South Africa's policy for the local integration of refugee populations. By removing the right to work and confining asylum-seekers to detention centres, it is assumed that the flow of asylum-seekers to the country will dry up. This, of course, ignores the growing evidence of the positive economic contribution of refugees and asylum-seekers who, under existing law, are permitted to pursue economic livelihoods. Denial of the existing right of refugees to seek permanent residence after five years in refugee status is further evidence of the desire to ensure that no refugee remains and is integrated into South African society.

International trends which increasingly stress the positive development impacts of refugee populations are being completely ignored.[79] Rather, the emphasis is on the "exceptionalism" of forced migrants and the need to craft a coercive, non-developmental approach to dealing with refugees. This represents a profound shift in the country's approach to refugee rights, protections, and associated international obligations; moving away from an integration approach towards a containment approach. While the new approach may appear to be a local response to intemperate local demands, it is part of a more global state-led trend that seeks to inhibit access to the physical territory and refugee protection systems of those countries through erecting physical, economic and social barriers to entry.[80] While there may be a belief that detention centres will reduce the flow of genuine asylum-seekers to South Africa, there remains a whole set of unanswered questions about whether there will be new policies that directly affect those who have refugee status. There is no indication whether those with refugee status will be denied the right to work, to self-employment, to freedom of movement, and to access health and educational services. Yet, they will not be given any additional resources and will be expected to pursue their own livelihoods, as at present.

To understand the challenges and obstacles that refugees face in securing these livelihoods, it is important to examine the policy and regulatory environment within which those in the informal sector try to survive. Refugees and asylum-seekers confront a formidable set of challenges in operating their informal enterprises in South African cities.[81] At best grudgingly tolerated, and at worst increasingly hounded out of communities by xenophobic mobs and violent entrepreneurship, those fleeing violence and persecution at home certainly do not find a safe haven in South Africa. It is arguable that one of the reasons why the state, and the police in particular, have failed to act against the perpetrators of xenophobic violence, with very low rates of arrest and prosecution, is that xenophobia does serve very practical ends. Not only does it make many South African communities spaces of fear for refugees and asylum-seekers, it also renders the country as a whole an undesirable destination for future refugees. As this report argues, xenophobic violence and police inaction are undoubtedly not the only difficulties that refugees face in the informal sector. South African city managers oscillate between benign neglect and active destruction of this vibrant and economically productive sector. Migrants who run informal enterprises have been major targets of a series of national, provincial and local-level "operations" designed to limit or eradicate their businesses from urban space. There is thus a fundamental contradiction between a refugee protection policy that demands self-reliance from refugees and informal sector policies that undermine self-reliance at every turn.

Restricting opportunities to pursue a livelihood in the country's informal sector also contributes to the general aim of making South Africa undesirable. A comparison of the draft and final Refugees Amendment Act suggests that the petitions and representations of human rights groups and refugee and migrant associations have had little or no impact in softening the legislation. Litigation in the courts is therefore likely to continue to be the most likely way to roll back draconian provisions. The courts have played an increasingly important role in securing the livelihoods of informal-sector operators in general, and migrant entrepreneurs in particular, in post-apartheid South Africa. Litigation has been one of the key sources of support to migrant entrepreneurs, highlighting the core contradiction between the rights enshrined in the South African Constitution, on the one hand, and the policies and actions of key government departments and officials, on the other. Protecting refugee rights is likely to continue to rely on a cohort of non-governmental organizations prioritizing migrant livelihood rights and being willing and able to pursue time-consuming and costly litigation on their behalf.

ENDNOTES

1   Amit (2011, 2012, 2015); Johnson (2015); Polzer Ngwato (2013).

2   DHA (2017).

3   Fiddian-Qasmiyeh et al. (2014).

4   Handmaker et al. (2011).

5   Handmaker (2001).

6   Amit (2011, 2015); Handmaker et al. (2011); Igglesden and Schreier (2011); Landau (2006).

7   Crush and Tevera (2010); Crush et al. (2015).

8   Polzer Ngwato (2013).

9   Gigaba (2016).

10   DHA (2017, p. 68).

11   Amit (2012).

12   Hassim et al. (2008).

13 Gordon (2016).

14 Crush et al. (2015).

15 Gordon (2016, p. 1).

16 Landau and Duponchel (2011, p. 19).

17 DHA (2017, p. 32).

18 Stupart (2016).

19 DHA (2017, p. 70).

20 Mah and Rivers (2016).

21 DHA (2017, pp. 69-70).

22 DHA (2017, p. 70).

23 Polzer Ngwato (2013).

24 DHA (2017, p. 45).

25 Carciotto (2016).

26 Washinyira (2012).

27 Tawodzera et al. (2015), Peberdy (2017).

28 Rogerson (2004, p. 765).

29 Devey et al. (2003, 2008).

30 Budlender et al. (2004); Chandra and Rajaratnam (2001); Skinner (2005).

31 Mbeki (2003).

32 Devey et al. (2006); du Toit and Neves (2007).

33 Devey et al. (2006, p. 242).

34 RSA (2006, p. 11).

35 NPC (2012).

36 NPC (2012, p. 121).

37 Rogerson (2016a, p.175).

38 DTI (2014).

39 DTI (2013).

40 DTI (2013, p.5).

41 Charman et al. (2013).

42 DTI (2013, p. 22).

43 DTI (2014, pp. 10, 22).

44 Ibid., p. 57.

45 Ibid., pp. 22-23.

46 Ibid., pp. 22.

47 Rogerson (2016a, p. 184).

48 City Press (2013).

49 Horn (2013, p. 2).

50 Crush et al. (2015, pp. 15-17).

51 Crush and Ramachandran (2015, p. 49).

52 PMG (2015).

53 Nicolson (2015).

54 Chivugare (2015).

55 Zwane (2014).

56 Magubane (2015).

57 Mazwai (2017).

58 Mazwai (2016).

59 KwaZulu-Natal Provincial Government (2011).

60 Western Cape Province (2014), Gauteng Province (2015).

61 Gauteng Province (2015, p. 45).

62 News 24 (2015).

63 Supreme Court (2014).

64 Supreme Court (2014, pp. 6-7).

65 Supreme Court (2014, p. 25).

66 City of Johannesburg (2009, p. 3).

67 City of Cape Town (2013, p. 8).

68 eThekwini Unicity Municipality (2001, p. 1).

69 Wafer (2014).

70 Zack (2015), Rogerson (2016b).

71 Constitutional Court (2014).

72 Bukasa (2014).

73 Zulu (2015).

74 Crush et al. (2015, p. 15).

75 Gastrow and Amit (2015).

76 Lund and Skinner (2004), Dobson and Skinner (2009).

77 Skinner (2010).

78 Dube et al. (2013).

79 UNHCR (2014), World Bank (2016).

80 Mountz (2013), Mountz et al. (2013).

81 Crush et al. (2015).

REFERENCES

1. Amit, R. (2011). "No Refuge: Flawed Status Determination and the Failures of South Africa's Refugee System to Provide Protection" *International Journal of Refugee Law* 23: 458-488.

2. Amit. R. (2012). *No Way In: Barriers to Access, Service and Administrative Justice at South Africa's Refugee Reception Offices*. ACMS Report, Johannesburg.

3. Amit, R. (2015). *Queue Here for Corruption: Measuring Irregularities in South Africa's Asylum System*. Report for LHR and ACMS, Johannesburg.

4. Budlender, D., Skinner C. and Valodia, I. (2004). *Budgets and the Informal Economy: An Analysis of the Impact of the Budget on Informal Workers in South Africa*. School of Development Studies Research Report, University of KwaZulu-Natal, Durban.

5. Bukasa, A. (2014). "Securing Sustainable Livelihoods: A Critical Assessment of the City of Cape Town's Approach to Inner City Street Trading" MA Thesis, University of Cape Town, Cape Town.

6. Carciotto, S. (2016). "Angolan Refugees in South Africa: Alternatives to Permanent Repatriation?" *African Human Mobility Review* 2: 362-382.

7. Chandra, V. and Rajaratnam, B. (2001). *Constraints to Growth and Employment in the Informal Sector: Evidence from the 1999 Informal Survey Firm* (Washington: World Bank).

8. Charman, A., Petersen, L. and Piper, L. (2013). "Enforced Informalisation: The Case of Liquor Retailers in South Africa" *Development Southern Africa* 30: 580-595.

9. Chivugare, B. (2015). "Army Closes Down Cape Town Station" *GroundUp* 22 June.

10. City of Cape Town (2013). *Informal Trading Policy 2013 (Policy Number 12664)*. Cape Town.

11. City of Johannesburg (2009). *Informal Trading Policy 2009.* Johannesburg.

12. City Press (2013). "Foreign-Owned Businesses Hampering Rural Growth – dti" At http://www.news24.com/Archives/City-Press/Foreign-owned-businesses-hampering-rural-growth-dti-20150429

13. Constitutional Court (2014). *South African Informal Traders Forum and Others v City of Johannesburg and Others; South African National Traders Retail Association v City of Johannesburg and Others* (CCT 173/13; CCT 174/14) [2014] ZACC 8; 2014 (6) BCLR 726 (CC); 2014 (4) SA 371 (CC) (4 April)

14. Crush, J. and Ramachandran, S. (2015). "Doing Business with Xenophobia" In J. Crush, A. Chikanda and C. Skinner (eds.), *Mean Streets: Migration, Xenophobia and Informality in South Africa* (Ottawa: IDRC and Cape Town: SAMP), pp. 25-59.

15. Crush, J. and Tevera, D. (eds.) (2010). *Zimbabwe's Exodus: Crisis, Migration, Survival.* Ottawa and Cape Town: IDRC and SAMP.

16. Crush, J., Chikanda, A. and Skinner, C. (eds.) 2015. *Mean Streets: Migration, Xenophobia and Informality in South Africa* (Ottawa: IDRC and Cape Town: SAMP).

17. Crush, J., Chikanda, A. and Tawodzera, G. (2016). "The Third Wave: Mixed Migration from Zimbabwe to South Africa" *Canadian Journal of African Studies* 49: 363-382.

18. Devey, R. Skinner, C and Valodia, I. (2003). "Human Resource Development in the Informal Economy" In A. Kraak and K. Press (eds.), *Human Resource Development Biennial Directory* (Cape Town: HSRC Press).

19. Devey, R., Skinner, C. and Valodia, I. (2006). "The State of the Informal Economy" In S. Buhlungu, J. Daniel, R. Southall and J. Lutchman (eds.), *The State of the Nation, 2005-2006* (Cape Town: HSRC Press).

20. Devey, R. Skinner, C and Valodia, I. (2008). "The Informal Economy" In A. Kraak and K. Press (eds.), *Human Resource Development Biennial Directory* (Cape Town: HSRC Press).

21. DHA (2017). *White Paper on International Migration to South Africa.* Department of Home Affairs, Pretoria.

22. Dobson, R. and Skinner, C. (2009). *Working in Warwick: Integrating Street Traders into Urban Plans* (Durban: University of KwaZulu-Natal).

23. DTI (2013). *The Draft Business Licensing Bill.* Pretoria: Department of Trade and Industry.

24. DTI (2014). *The National Informal Business Upliftment Strategy (NIBUS).* Pretoria: Department of Trade and Industry.

25. Du Toit, A. and Neves, D. (2007). "In Search of South Africa's 'Second Economy'" *Africanus* 37: 145-174.

26. Dube, G., Mkhize, S. and Skinner, C. (2013). *Informal Economy Monitoring Study: Street Vendors in Durban, South Africa.* Inclusive Cities Research Report, WIEGO, Manchester.

27. eThekwini Unicity Municipality (2001). Durban's Informal Economic Policy. At http://www.durban.gov.za/City_Services/BST_MU/Documents/Informal_Economy_Policy.pdf

28. Fiddian-Qasmiyeh, E., Loescher, G., Long, K. and Sigona, N. (eds.) (2014). *The Oxford Handbook of Refugee and Forced Migration Studies* (Oxford: OUP).

29. Gastrow, V. and Amit, R. (2015). "The Role of Migrant Traders in Local Economies : A Case Study of Somali Spaza Shops in Cape Town" In J. Crush, A. Chikanda and C. Skinner (eds.), *Mean Streets: Migration, Xenophobia and Informality in South Africa* (Ottawa: IDRC and Cape Town: SAMP).

30. Gauteng Province (2015). *Gauteng Informal Business Upliftment Strategy.* Economic Development Department.

31. Gigaba, M. (2016). "Address by Minister Gigaba at the Department of Home Affairs World Refugee Day" At: http://www.dha.gov.za/index.php/statements-speeches/812-address-by-minister-gigaba-at-the-department-of-home-affairs-world-refugee-day-event-at-the-catholic-archdiocese-of-johannesburg-on-02-june-2016

32. Gordon, S. (2016). "Welcoming Refugees in the Rainbow Nation: Contemporary Attitudes Towards Refugees in South Africa" *African Geographical Review* 35: 1-17.

33. Handmaker, J. (2001). "No Easy Walk: Advancing Refugee Protection in South Africa" *Africa Today* 48: 91-113.

34. Handmaker, J., de la Hunt, L. and Klaaren, J. (eds.) (2011). *Advancing Refugee Protection in South Africa 2nd Edition* (Oxford: Berghahn Books).

35. Hassim, S., Kupe, T. and Worby, E. (eds.) (2008). *Go Home or Die Here: Violence, Xenophobia and the Reinvention of Difference in South Africa* (Johannesburg: Wits University Press).

36. Horn, P. (2013). "Submission on behalf of StreetNet International on the Licensing of Businesses Bill 2013" At http://www.streetnet.org.za/docs/letters/2013/en/Bill2013submission.pdf.

37. Igglesden, V. and Schreier, T. (2011). "Expanding the Protection Space for Refugees in South Africa" Refugee Rights Unit Working Paper 2, University of Cape Town.

38. Johnson, C. (2015). "Failed Asylum Seekers in South Africa: Policy and Practice" *African Human Mobility Review* 1: 201-228.

39. KwaZulu-Natal Provincial Government (2011). *Policy for the Informal Economy of Kwa-Zulu-Natal,* Department of Economic Development and Tourism, Durban.

40. Landau, L. (2006). "Protection and Dignity in Johannesburg: Shortcomings of South Africa's Urban Refugee Policy" *Journal of Refugee Studies* 19: 308-327.

41. Landau, L. and Duponchel, M. (2011). "Laws, Policies, or Social Position? Capabilities and the Determinants of Effective Protection in Four African Cities" *Journal of Refugee Studies* 24: 1-22.

42. Lund, F. and Skinner, C. (2004). "Integrating the Informal Economy in Urban Planning and Governance: A Case Study of the Process of Policy Development in Durban, South Africa" *International Development Planning Review* 26: 431-456.

43. Magubane, K. (2015). "Reveal Trade Secrets, Minister Tells Foreigners" *Business Day* 28 January.

44. Mah, K. and Rivers, P. (2016). "Refugee Housing Without Exception" *Space and Culture* 19: 390-405.

45. Mazwai, T. (2016). "Time to Confront Home Truths" *Business Report* 24 May.

46. Mazwai, T. (2017). "The Great Township Business Summit" *Business Report* 13 June.

47. Mbeki, T. (2003). "Address to the National Council of Provinces, 11 November" At http://www.sahistory.org.za/archive/address-national-council-provinces-11-november-2003

48. Mountz, A. (2013). "Shrinking Spaces of Asylum: Vanishing Points Where Geography Is Used to Inhibit Access to Asylum" *Journal of Human Rights* 19: 29-50

49. Mountz, A., Coddington, K., Catania, R. and Loyd, J. (2013). "Conceptualizing Detention: Mobility Containment Bordering and Exclusion" *Progress in Human Geography* 37: 522-541.

50. NPC (2012). *National Development Plan: Vision for 2030, Our Future – Make it Work* (Pretoria: National Planning Commission).

51. News24 (2015). "MEC to Uplift Smaller Businesses" *News24* 14 May.

52. Nicolson, G. (2015). "Parliamentary Report on Xenophobic Violence Talks a Lot, Says Very Little" *Daily Maverick* 24 November.

53. Peberdy, S. (2017). *Competition or Co-operation? South African and Migrant Entrepreneurs in Johannesburg.* SAMP Migration Policy Series No. 75, Cape Town.

54. PMG (2015). "Inter-Ministerial Committee Briefing" At https://pmg.org.za/committee-meeting/21805/

55. Polzer Ngwato, T. (2013). *Policy Shifts in the South African Asylum System.* Report for LHR and ACMS, Johannesburg.

56. RSA (2006). *Accelerated Shared Growth Initiative of South Africa.* At http://www.daff.gov.za/docs/GenPub/asgisa.pdf

57. Rogerson, C. (2004). "The Impact of the South African Government's SMME Programmes: A Ten Year Review" *Development Southern Africa* 21: 765-784.

58. Rogerson, C. (2016a). "South Africa's Informal Economy: Reframing Debates in National Policy" *Local Economy* 31: 172-186.

59. Rogerson, C. (2016b). "Progressive Rhetoric, Ambiguous Policy Pathways: Street Trading in Inner-City Johannesburg, South Africa" *Local Economy* 31: 204-218.

60. Skinner, C. (2005). *Constraints to Growth and Employment: Evidence from the Informal Economy.* School of Development Studies Research Report No. 65, University of KwaZulu-Natal, Durban.

61. Skinner, C. (2010). "Challenging City Imaginaries: Street Traders' Struggles in Warwick Junction" *Agenda* 23: 101-109.

62. Stupart, R. (2016). "Is South Africa Home to More Than a Million Asylum Seekers? The Numbers Don't Add Up" *Africa Check* 15 August.

63. Supreme Court (2014). *Somali Association of South Africa and Others v Limpopo Department of Economic Development Environment and Tourism and Others* (48/2014) [2014] ZASCA 143; 2015 (1) SA 151 (SCA); [2014] 4 All SA 600 (SCA) (26 September).

64. Tawodzera, G., Chikanda, A., Crush, J. and Tengeh, R. (2015). *International Migrants and Refugees in Cape Town's Informal Economy.* SAMP Migration Policy Series No. 70, Cape Town.

65. UNHCR (2014). *Global Strategy for Livelihoods* (Geneva: UNHCR).

66. Wafer (2014). "Informality and the Spaces of Civil Society in Post-Apartheid Johannesburg" In C. Gabay and C. Death (eds.), *Critical Perspectives on African Politics* (New York: Routledge).

67. Washinyira, T. (2012). "Asylum Seekers Struggle as FNB Freezes Their Accounts" *GroundUp* 5 December.

68. World Bank (2016). *Forcibly Displaced: Toward a Development Approach Supporting Refugees, the Internally Displaced, and Their Hosts* (Washington DC: World Bank).

69. Western Cape Province (2014). *Draft Informal Sector Framework*, Cape Town.

70. Zack, T. (2015). "Making an Area Hot: Interrupting Trade in an Ethnic Enclave in Johannesburg's Inner City" In J. Crush, A. Chikanda and C. Skinner (eds.), *Mean Streets: Migration, Xenophobia and Informality in South Africa* (Ottawa: IDRC and Cape Town: SAMP).

71. Zulu, T. (2015). "Interchange for the Informal Market? An Investigation of the Nature of the Nolungile Station Upgrades in Khayelitsha, Cape Town and Their Implications for Informal Traders" MA Thesis, University of Cape Town.

72. Zwane, T. (2014). "Spazas: Talking Shop is Good for Business" *Mail & Guardian* 7 November.

MIGRATION POLICY SERIES

1 *Covert Operations: Clandestine Migration, Temporary Work and Immigration Policy in South Africa* (1997) ISBN 1-874864-51-9

2 *Riding the Tiger: Lesotho Miners and Permanent Residence in South Africa* (1997) ISBN 1-874864-52-7

3 *International Migration, Immigrant Entrepreneurs and South Africa's Small Enterprise Economy* (1997) ISBN 1-874864-62-4

4 *Silenced by Nation Building: African Immigrants and Language Policy in the New South Africa* (1998) ISBN 1-874864-64-0

5 *Left Out in the Cold? Housing and Immigration in the New South Africa* (1998) ISBN 1-874864-68-3

6 *Trading Places: Cross-Border Traders and the South African Informal Sector* (1998) ISBN 1-874864-71-3

7 *Challenging Xenophobia: Myth and Realities about Cross-Border Migration in Southern Africa* (1998) ISBN 1-874864-70-5

8 *Sons of Mozambique: Mozambican Miners and Post-Apartheid South Africa* (1998) ISBN 1-874864-78-0

9 *Women on the Move: Gender and Cross-Border Migration to South Africa* (1998) ISBN 1-874864-82-9

10 *Namibians on South Africa: Attitudes Towards Cross-Border Migration and Immigration Policy* (1998) ISBN 1-874864-84-5

11 *Building Skills: Cross-Border Migrants and the South African Construction Industry* (1999) ISBN 1-874864-84-5

12 *Immigration & Education: International Students at South African Universities and Technikons* (1999) ISBN 1-874864-89-6

13 *The Lives and Times of African Immigrants in Post-Apartheid South Africa* (1999) ISBN 1-874864-91-8

14 *Still Waiting for the Barbarians: South African Attitudes to Immigrants and Immigration* (1999) ISBN 1-874864-91-8

15 *Undermining Labour: Migrancy and Sub-Contracting in the South African Gold Mining Industry* (1999) ISBN 1-874864-91-8

16 *Borderline Farming: Foreign Migrants in South African Commercial Agriculture* (2000) ISBN 1-874864-97-7

17 *Writing Xenophobia: Immigration and the Press in Post-Apartheid South Africa* (2000) ISBN 1-919798-01-3

18 *Losing Our Minds: Skills Migration and the South African Brain Drain* (2000) ISBN 1-919798-03-x

19 *Botswana: Migration Perspectives and Prospects* (2000) ISBN 1-919798-04-8

20 *The Brain Gain: Skilled Migrants and Immigration Policy in Post-Apartheid South Africa* (2000) ISBN 1-919798-14-5

21 *Cross-Border Raiding and Community Conflict in the Lesotho-South African Border Zone* (2001) ISBN 1-919798-16-1

22 *Immigration, Xenophobia and Human Rights in South Africa* (2001) ISBN 1-919798-30-7

23 *Gender and the Brain Drain from South Africa* (2001) ISBN 1-919798-35-8

24 *Spaces of Vulnerability: Migration and HIV/AIDS in South Africa* (2002) ISBN 1-919798-38-2

25 *Zimbabweans Who Move: Perspectives on International Migration in Zimbabwe* (2002) ISBN 1-919798-40-4

26 *The Border Within: The Future of the Lesotho-South African International Boundary* (2002) ISBN 1-919798-41-2

27 *Mobile Namibia: Migration Trends and Attitudes* (2002) ISBN 1-919798-44-7

28 *Changing Attitudes to Immigration and Refugee Policy in Botswana* (2003) ISBN 1-919798-47-1

29 *The New Brain Drain from Zimbabwe* (2003) ISBN 1-919798-48-X

30 *Regionalizing Xenophobia? Citizen Attitudes to Immigration and Refugee Policy in Southern Africa* (2004) ISBN 1-919798-53-6

31 *Migration, Sexuality and HIV/AIDS in Rural South Africa* (2004) ISBN 1-919798-63-3

32 *Swaziland Moves: Perceptions and Patterns of Modern Migration* (2004) ISBN 1-919798-67-6

33 *HIV/AIDS and Children's Migration in Southern Africa* (2004) ISBN 1-919798-70-6

34 *Medical Leave: The Exodus of Health Professionals from Zimbabwe* (2005) ISBN 1-919798-74-9

35 *Degrees of Uncertainty: Students and the Brain Drain in Southern Africa* (2005) ISBN 1-919798-84-6

36 *Restless Minds: South African Students and the Brain Drain* (2005) ISBN 1-919798-82-X

37 *Understanding Press Coverage of Cross-Border Migration in Southern Africa since 2000* (2005) ISBN 1-919798-91-9

38 *Northern Gateway: Cross-Border Migration Between Namibia and Angola* (2005) ISBN 1-919798-92-7

39 *Early Departures: The Emigration Potential of Zimbabwean Students* (2005) ISBN 1-919798-99-4

40 *Migration and Domestic Workers: Worlds of Work, Health and Mobility in Johannesburg* (2005) ISBN 1-920118-02-0

41 *The Quality of Migration Services Delivery in South Africa* (2005) ISBN 1-920118-03-9

42 *States of Vulnerability: The Future Brain Drain of Talent to South Africa* (2006) ISBN 1-920118-07-1

43 *Migration and Development in Mozambique: Poverty, Inequality and Survival* (2006) ISBN 1-920118-10-1

44 *Migration, Remittances and Development in Southern Africa* (2006) ISBN 1-920118-15-2

45 *Medical Recruiting: The Case of South African Health Care Professionals* (2007) ISBN 1-920118-47-0

46 *Voices From the Margins: Migrant Women's Experiences in Southern Africa* (2007) ISBN 1-920118-50-0

47 *The Haemorrhage of Health Professionals From South Africa: Medical Opinions* (2007) ISBN 978-1-920118-63-1

48 *The Quality of Immigration and Citizenship Services in Namibia* (2008) ISBN 978-1-920118-67-9

49 *Gender, Migration and Remittances in Southern Africa* (2008) ISBN 978-1-920118-70-9

50 *The Perfect Storm: The Realities of Xenophobia in Contemporary South Africa* (2008) ISBN 978-1-920118-71-6

51 *Migrant Remittances and Household Survival in Zimbabwe* (2009) ISBN 978-1-920118-92-1

52 *Migration, Remittances and 'Development' in Lesotho* (2010) ISBN 978-1-920409-26-5

53 *Migration-Induced HIV and AIDS in Rural Mozambique and Swaziland* (2011) ISBN 978-1-920409-49-4

54 *Medical Xenophobia: Zimbabwean Access to Health Services in South Africa* (2011) ISBN 978-1-920409-63-0

55 *The Engagement of the Zimbabwean Medical Diaspora* (2011) ISBN 978-1-920409-64-7

56 *Right to the Classroom: Educational Barriers for Zimbabweans in South Africa* (2011) ISBN 978-1-920409-68-5

57 *Patients Without Borders: Medical Tourism and Medical Migration in Southern Africa* (2012) ISBN 978-1-920409-74-6

58 *The Disengagement of the South African Medical Diaspora* (2012) ISBN 978-1-920596-00-2

59 *The Third Wave: Mixed Migration from Zimbabwe to South Africa* (2012) ISBN 978-1-920596-01-9

60 *Linking Migration, Food Security and Development* (2012) ISBN 978-1-920596-02-6

61 *Unfriendly Neighbours: Contemporary Migration from Zimbabwe to Botswana* (2012) ISBN 978-1-920596-16-3

62 *Heading North: The Zimbabwean Diaspora in Canada* (2012) ISBN 978-1-920596-03-3

63 *Dystopia and Disengagement: Diaspora Attitudes Towards South Africa* (2012) ISBN 978-1-920596-04-0

64 *Soft Targets: Xenophobia, Public Violence and Changing Attitudes to Migrants in South Africa after May 2008* (2013) ISBN 978-1-920596-05-7

65 *Brain Drain and Regain: Migration Behaviour of South African Medical Professionals* (2014) ISBN 978-1-920596-07-1

66 *Xenophobic Violence in South Africa: Denialism, Minimalism, Realism* (2014) ISBN 978-1-920596-08-8

67 *Migrant Entrepreneurship Collective Violence and Xenophobia in South Africa* (2014) ISBN 978-1-920596-09-5

68 *Informal Migrant Entrepreneurship and Inclusive Growth in South Africa, Zimbabwe and Mozambique* (2015) ISBN 978-1-920596-10-1

69 *Calibrating Informal Cross-Border Trade in Southern Africa* (2015) ISBN 978-1-920596-13-2

www.ingramcontent.com/pod-product-compliance
Lightning Source LLC
Chambersburg PA
CBHW080135270326
41926CB00021B/4491